MY WALK AT SOTTO
By: Jed Ronald R. Filoteo
With Introduction and
Footnotes by Malou Alfaro-Alorro

INTRODUCTION
By Malou Alfaro-Alorro

In July, 2016 my daughter was confined in one of the private hospitals in Cebu City, Central Philippines due to acute dehydration. This was caused by ill-prepared macaroni soup she ate from a fast food chain in one of the malls. We stayed on the second floor in a private room in the hospital. The 3 days of confinement actually lengthened to another 3 days due to a serious oversight by the medical team in the reading of a blood pressure caused by a defective apparatus used by the medical personnel. There was only one blood pressure instrument used for the whole second floor in the said hospital. The instrument looked old, rubbery and failed registering the right reading. This was corrected when I bought my own apparatus and requested for another instrument from the Cardio department to compare blood pressure readings with that of the second floor. The same readings were registered from the apparatus I bought and from the Cardio department. I recommended that the old blood pressure apparatus on the second floor be changed. I made an Incident Report on the matter and endorsed it to Management and the Department of Health (DOH) for investigation.

Other than this oversight, what struck me during this length of stay with my daughter in the hospital was the visit of a colleague at the Cebu City Hall, Jed Ronald Filoteo. He came into the room, talked to me and my daughter about our faith and prayed for healing. His presence comforted me from the stress attending to a loved one with an ailment. He said that he has been active in the apostolate of hospital visits since 1996. He stopped in 2003 to attend to his family as he had small children and was back in 2015, last year. He said he wrote his thoughts and reflections on paper and I offered to read them. True enough, he gave me a manuscript of his witnessing and his reflections.

The words are his. It is a raw language borne from an English education in the Philippines. It is manifest of the energy and the spirit that beholds the man when he takes time to visit the sick in the hospitals. Jed Ronald Filoteo's reflections in this book give us glimpses of the man who is deeply passionate in his apostolate in hospital visits. Sotto is his Sunday stop, his main turf- the wards of Sotto. It refers to the provincial hospital in Cebu, Central Philippines – Vicente Sotto Memorial Medical Center (VSMMC).

In 1911, this hospital was constructed during the American Occupation and was named Hospital del Sur. On January 2, 1913 by virtue of Republic Act No. 2725, Hospital del Sur was renamed as Southern Islands Hospital with a 30- bed capacity. It was also in the same law that the Secretary of the Interior was authorized to establish the School of Nursing in the Southern Islands Hospital. On May 21, 1992 by virtue of Republic Act 7258, Southern Islands Hospital was renamed Vicente Sotto Memorial Medical Center (VSMMC) in honor of former Philippine Senator Vicente Yap Sotto who was known to author the Press Freedom Law, also known as the Sotto Law.

When I was in college, way back in the 1980's I was part of this team who volunteers for outreach programs. These would include teaching catechism in public schools, visiting the sick in hospitals, visiting prisoners in jails, meeting with members of the urban poor, integrating with farmers in rural communities or with fisher folks in costal villages.

Consequently, for a long time in-between from then and now, I have been in and out of hospitals at some point through the years. And I have seldom encountered people who seek out the sick, visit them, console them; be with them, assist them, facilitate some errands for them, or simply attend to them in their loneliness and aloneness.

Typically a Catholic, Jed Ronald Filoteo immerses into the teachings of his faith as he believed them. Although some of his admonitions in this witnessing are strict and perhaps, filled with religiosity. He is honest in sharing that through these years, he has lived away from drugs and other vices in his younger years and as a mature man, he now seeks guidance in his Christian faith and endorses the rites of the Catholic Church.

This book shares with us the transformation of a worldly man to a man with an apostolic mission – the hospital visitation for the sick; a witnessing of the lives of people in their sick beds. The Philippines' public hospitals are filled with poor people who are staying in wards and emergency rooms. Health care in these hospitals is so wanting because budgets are so small. Yet, people like Jed Ronald Filoteo, offer hope and enlightenment, who pray for healing, peace, faith and conversion and as readers we bear witness to the stories narrated in this book.

He has paved the installing of a resident priest at the hospital in Sotto. In one of the pages in this book, he narrates how he went to the Archbishop's Palace, met the Cardinal and requested for a resident priest. This was attended a month after.

He has lived a simple life. His family supports him. He is happy in what he is doing on Sundays. And he prays that more people will share his apostolate to bring consolation, depth, joy and healing to the sick in hospitals.

Jed and wife, Chona in front of Vicente Sotto Memorial Medical Center.

MY WALK AT SOTTO
By: Jed Ronald R. Filoteo

In 1994, I went to an Asian country with an associate upon the invitation of a British friend. We did plastic castings. I was paired with an elder British national who was a Protestant working on the 24th floor in the same building. I noticed that adjacent to the building where we were working was a Chinese temple adorned with statues of Chinese deities and people were celebrating their feast that week. There was a dragon dance, explosion of firecrackers and offering of food. I told my British friend in jest to stop working and partake of the food they are offering. He declined because according to him they were worshipping another god. He added that there is only one God to worship and that is Jesus Christ. I asked him, "Who will teach them about Jesus Christ?" He replied, "It's you and me." I replied, "No way! That's the work of the missionaries." He shot back, "It's you and me. As baptized Christians, we are mandated to preach the good news of salvation."

Wonder of all wonders, two years later, I was walking the wards at Vicente Sotto Memorial Medical Center (VSMMC)[1] doing hospital apostolate.

In 1996, I gave my life to Jesus during my initiation in the Life and Spirit Seminar (LSS)[2] of the *Bato sa Gugma ni Kristo* (a religious

---

[1] Vicente Sotto Memorial Medical Center (VSMMC) was established in 1911 during the American Occupation in the Philippines and was formerly known then as Hospital del Sur. In 1913, it was renamed Southern Islands Hospital and in 1992, it was renamed after Senator Vicente Yap Sotto, (April 18, 1877 – May 28, 1950) the main author of the Press Freedom Law (now known as the Sotto Law, Republic Act No. 53)

[2] Life in the Spirit Seminar or LSS is commonly used by Catholic groups in their

community of lay people) at the Cebu City Metropolitan Cathedral. I attended the three night's seminar together with my girlfriend who became my future wife. It was my *kumpare's*[3] insistence that made me attend the seminar. I reasoned out that this was useless; and told him I attended this before and it did not do me any good. But he was so bent on letting me attend. After the activity, I did an in-depth study on Bible passages and readings from religious articles in the mornings. My father commented, instead of simply studying God's Word, why not accompany him to VSMMC preaching the good news of salvation?

I went with him that afternoon. He told me to listen as he conversed with a patient. After administering to the second patient, he directed me to talk to the other patient. This was the start of my hospital apostolate career. I didn't find it hard to do because I had undergone a month-long training on One-on-One Evangelization. Thanks to the Siao couple who spearheaded the said activity. Our practicum was held at Sitio Bato in Barangay[4] Ermita. I remembered, we were prayed-over by a priest after a Sunday mass and we were sent off as evangelizers.

I was with my Dad at VSMMC for 6 years. He ceased doing his work as 'fishers of men' when he was bedridden for 6 years due to heart attack and prostate cancer. He passed away doing this ministry for 19 years serving two public hospitals, the Vicente

---

renewal of faith. The seminar offers basic presentation and teachings of the Gospel.

[3] Kumpare in the Philippine language means a male friend or buddy, usually one who is taken as a sponsor during a child's baptism, a godfather.

[4] Barangay in the Philippines is the most basic unit in local government. It literally means a community of people. For example, Cebu City has 80 barangays in the southern and northern parts, including the mountains and the coastal areas.

Sotto Memorial Medical Center (VSMMC) and the Cebu City Medical Center (CCMC).

With my apostolate in hospital visitation, I crafted a module: an opening, middle and ending statements in my approach with patients. I approach a patient with a wide grin. I am very cordial in my dealings and adopt a non-confrontational style and refrain from debates in my conversation.

Below is the format that I follow:

a.) I introduce myself. I tell them that I am from the Cebu Metropolitan Cathedral so they will not be surprised of my intention which is religious in nature.

b.) I ask them if one is Catholic and if so, I inquire if one has misgivings and blames God why s/he is confined in the hospital.

c.) If one says yes, I say s/he should not blame God for the misery. One should be happy being alive. Others have died on their way to the hospital while others who were earlier confined have also died. They have been covered with white cloth ready for disposal to the morgue. Their physical existence have ended and did not have more time mending their lives, seeking forgiveness and having more opportunity walking with God. I tell them, "But you, you should rejoice! You are still alive. You have time to seek forgiveness; change your life from bad to good; have the opportunity to help others and live a good Christian life."

If one is non- Catholic, I inquire how they are coping in their relationship with God, the frequency in their Church attendance and encourage them to have a good relationship with others, stop committing sin and continue serving God.

d.) I gauge their religious life by asking:

Are you married and solemnized by the Church? If yes, that's good. If not, I explain to them the importance of Holy Matrimony. It's a sacrament and without it, both are living in sin. I tell them to avail of a mass wedding[5] offered in the community if the hindrance is expenses. If one or both are married and separated, I tell them to have this annulled by the Church where the process has been simplified and is not as costly. One wonders why our prayers remain unanswered because both are in the state of sin due to an illicit relationship. We have to get rid of the obstacle so the grace from God will flow into our life. We should refrain from taking Holy Communion if we have not been accorded with a church wedding.

e.) I inquire if they have been to Church and when was the last confession? And the status of their prayer life? I tell them, we have been remiss in our relationship with God due to the busyness of our work, our priorities, constant fun and vices. There are times when we forget to pray, thank Him, neglect Sunday mass and not having confession. But God does not forget us. He loves us! He

---

[5] There are mass weddings sponsored by local government units (LGUs) in the Philippines. In Cebu City, this is usually held in September and budgets include appropriations for the ceremony and the feast. The couple spends for their wardrobe. Usually, there are over a hundred couples who get married in a single ceremony. A mass wedding is a project launched by the local governments for Catholic couples who have been living together for years (common-law) who have children.

allows things to happen such as trials, sickness, problems and accidents. This will enable us to call on Him. He wants us to have Him as part of our daily lives as we lead Christian lives.

f.) I explain that in what we lack, we add. If we are not going to Mass, we resolve by attending Sunday masses. If we lack confession, we go back to the confessional; if we lack prayers, we pray daily because this is the only way we can commute with our Creator and we do the good works of mercy for others. Most important of all is not to commit sin. We have to pay for every sin we commit and this is very painful. We cannot say nobody is watching. Somebody up there sees us. Nothing is hidden and everything is known to Him. The mischievous child runs when the father spanks him but when God spanks us, it's a sure hit. I tell them to mend broken relationships with others because we have a loving and forgiving God. I encourage them to become members of any religious organizations in the church to deepen their faith.

g.) After my talk, I give confessional guides and rosaries. I encourage them to pray the Rosary daily. I remind them it's a special devotion done in 20 minutes imploring the help of Mama Mary, our Mother of Perpetual Help. If this cannot be finished in the morning, this can be continued in the afternoon or evening. I remind them, if Mama Mary declined the invitation of being the Mother of God, Jesus would have not have walked this earth. She is our Mother, our intercessor in heaven. I tell them, if you have experienced the love of your mother, why not experience the love of the mother of Christ?

Reflection:

I am aware that the enemy is patiently waiting for those who will die, interested solely in their souls, especially those distant from God. Here I am walking in the wards at Sotto doing hospital apostolate. My mission is to remind them that there is a loving God who knows, loves us and cares for us. I inspire them and tell them what a beautiful world we have in God's hands. I tell them to repent, change their lives and live a Christian life. One has to prepare for this kind of ministry, aware that the enemy is the most powerful in a world capable of doing harm. I pray the rosary daily, read Bible verses, and spend time in the prayer room prior to attending mass before going to the hospital. I refrain from committing sin, doing bad things. I seek the help of the Holy Spirit, Mama Mary, St. Michael the Archangel, all the angels and saints for intervention, asking guidance where He wants me to go, praying that whoever I preach with their hearts and minds will be receptive to the words of God.

There are those who are hard to approach unwilling to hear God's message. I remember the passage when Jesus instructed his disciples to shake off the dust from their sandals and leave when they are rejected. My repose is different. Instead of shaking the dust from my shoes, I pray for this person to be given another opportunity hearing God's word the soonest and will have a change of heart embracing God's love.

I ask God to take care of my needs in the continuous supply of rosaries and guides; confessional guides, budget for fares and snacks so my work will not be hampered by any lack of it.

I pray no distractions will occur when conversing with a patient such as a nurse who appears administering injection, check on vital signs, change dextrose[6], or cleaning wounds.

I realize my age is fast approaching its twilight. I did not achieve title, fame and fortune that everyone wants to have. I didn't have the opportunity of amassing wealth, possessing cars, acquiring houses, real estate and condominium; enjoying a luxurious lifestyle. I'm aware the things of this world will pass. I'm doing a different kind of investment not popular in this world's standard. It's an investment doing the works of mercy through hospital apostolate. I am trustful God will be gracious to people doing His work. When our time will come, God will be asking us," What have you done for me and others?" If we have fulfilled what He has destined for us, He tells us, "Come my faithful servant, I have a room for you." I pray everyone will be given the opportunity doing their share in the service of the Lord and to others.

There are others confined in the hospital revealing they were catechists, members of charismatic groups[7], lectors, lay ministers, members of Youth for Christ and other religious organizations. They reveal they have been inactive and have backslide. I remind them, plenty are called; few are chosen. I tell them they are the chosen ones and encourage them to continue serving God. I remind them their confinement is a wake-up call from Him who wants us to continue what we started.

There was a male patient from the southern part of Cebu who was a government employee. While listening to my talk, he confided that he used to be a lay minister[8] and became inactive. I

---

[6] Dextrose is an older chemical name for d-glucose; it's commonly used in the Philippines to refer to glucose solutions administered intravenously for fluid or replacement of nutrients.

[7] A charismatic group in the Philippines refers to a community that takes off from the Charismatic Movement, which is the international trend of historically mainstream congregations adopting beliefs and practices in the use of spiritual gifts (charismata).

told him to reflect on his confinement and asked if he missed serving God. I shared the story of a saint who would rather touch the hand of a priest rather than that of an angel because by doing so, he touches the body of Christ. I told him how blessed he is touching the body of Christ and encouraged him to continue serving the Lord.

One time, I encountered two female patients from different provinces who were acting strangely. Their beds were separated and they were tied to the sides. Both were shouting; talking in different language and had fierce-looking eyes. I found out that they were subjected to quack[9] healing before admitted to the hospital. I was not prepared for this kind of case, so I left. When descending from the second floor, I felt dizzy as if the world was spinning. I held on to the railings so I won't fall. I prayed to God for help and protection. I slowly inched my way to the direction of another hospital, the Cebu Doctor's Hospital and went directly to the chapel. I prayed the chaplet[10] until my senses came back to normal. I thanked God as I realized I was under attack by a negative spiritual force which inflicted those women. I told a priest. Fr. Monic, who went to the place the next day and cited prayers of deliverance.

There was a male patient; he was 40 years old who was diagnosed with leukemia and had limited time to live. I found out that he was working for a known priest in a southern town in Cebu and

---

[8] A lay minister is a member of Christian denominations who are not full-time paid clergy, or not ordained clergy, but who assist in performing the same or similar functions.

[9] Quack healing is common practice in some rural communities in the Philippines. Some practitioners use herbals and oils that have been blessed during the Lenten season. Others exorcise the presence of evil spirits or lost and souls who have not been prayed over.

[10] A chaplet is a Christian set of prayer beads intended for personal devotions asking for intercessions from Mother Mary, the saints and angels.

was assigned in the church as head in the administration office. I told him I know of friends working in the church who sometimes do not attend Mass. I also learned he was in-charge of all money matters and inquired if he had used some money for his personal needs. There and then, he broke down, admitting his remiss in not attending Mass, not having confession, and admitting of using the money for his personal use. I requested he seek confession considering that the hospital has an in-house chaplain. I told him to seek God for there is still time and God is always ready accepting repentant hearts even among the greatest sinners.

I was previously employed with a Hospital Medical Organization (HMO) as Liaison Officer dealing with doctors, hospitals and patients in four private hospitals in the city. This was an opportunity of reminding people of God's love, mercy and healing.

There was a female patient diagnosed with cancer. She was a supervisor in one of the big department stores in the city. She was known to be mean, haughty and hard on her co-employees. She was the eyes and ears of management, instrumental in the non-renewal of personnel employment. One time, she went to our company's laboratory for diagnostic checkup. She was furious when not immediately attended to by our staff. One of our lady technicians commented, "How can she still be in a rage when she has stage-four cancer?"

I visited her when she was confined in a private hospital. I inquired if she had undergone confession, aware that she is Catholic. She replied not having one. She inquired if I was connected with the Church. I said, yes. She requested that I prayed-over[11] her. I readily agreed. When I prayed asking God's

---

[11] To pray over means to lay hands offering prayers. This is very common in the

forgiveness of her sins, she started crying in a loud voice which could be heard outside the room. Her intense loud wailing made me numb, confused and I did not know what to do. I was not prepared how to respond, so I slipped out of the room. The next day, I was reprimanded by my manager of the incident as I told her what happened. Upon reflection, I realized that I should not have left the patient. I should have embraced her as a child of God, reminding her of His love, telling her to offer her fears, heaviness of heart and the darkness in her soul. I should have prayed for God's mercy unlocking the chains of sin and guilt in her life. I should have offered her to God imploring His mercy, pardon and healing. I should have prayed for love, comfort and lasting peace in her heart. I should have stayed with her in the saddest moment of her life until her crying ceased. A week later, she died. It was a lesson I learned.

One time, I served a Letter of Authority (LOA) to a patient confined in a private hospital covered by our company. He was more than 60 years old. I had the opportunity talking to him about God. He interrupted me and told me there is no God. He told me the issue of God is all business; the reason many have become millionaires. He told me he was a retired accountant. One time, he was told by his Chinese boss who was about to die that the boss will come back if there is God and he will tell him about it. He said that four years had passed; his boss has not appeared to him. I respected his views and left.

Three days later, I went back to the same ward attending to another patient. Upon seeing me, he called me, and asked if I was the same person who told him about God. He told me that he had been dreaming of his dead son who passed away 10 years ago, every three o'clock early morning and in the afternoon,

---

Philippines especially in cases that need healing and to solve problems.

successively for the past days. His wife told him we all have a spirit and his son is sending him a message that there is life after death. I told him the significance of the three o'clock time as the time when our Lord died. I saw the pastor of the hospital who was my friend and requested he administer to the patient. I had to leave and report back to the office because it was late in the afternoon. I was grateful of his renewed faith.

She was my neighbor during our childhood days. I remember she hit me with a stone hurting my forehead which required stitches. I did not see her for quite a time when she transferred to Subic.[12] I heard she got married, got separated and had relationships with other men and had children. I met her when she was back in Cebu settled with another man together with her children. I told her about renewing our life with the Lord and she told me as couple, they had undergone the Christian Life Program (CLP) upon the invitation of a religious community. I encouraged her to go on with her commitment with the Lord.

Several months had passed; I served an LOA to a patient confined in a private hospital at the Pediatrics Section. As I was about to leave the hospital, I didn't know why I was drawn to two stairs going up to the Gynecology Section. There I saw her, my former neighbor confined in bed. She was so surprised seeing me. She told me she had cervical cancer and had a few days to live. She told me she had undergone confession. I told her this is the time for self-examination, to seek God's love and mercy and offer our pain to Him. I told her all the sufferings we have in this world is incomparable to God's goodness in the next world. I prayed-over,

---

[12] Subic Bay Freeport Zone (SBFZ), which is known simply as Subic Bay is the Philippines' first successful case of a military base converted through volunteerism into a tax- and duty-free zone similar to Hong Kong and Singapore, operated and managed by the Subic Bay Metropolitan Authority or SBMA.

stayed an hour with her and left. I learned that she passed away two days later. But I was grateful that I shared with her a renewed faith.

There were persons I visited who were survivors of suicide. From what I gathered from my conversations with them, they decided ending their lives due to failed relationships, frustrations, dejection with their jobs and business opportunities, gravity of illness, and fear of being reprimanded for grave offenses. I told them they are fortunate being alive for God has a purpose and reason for their lives. I asked them to start a new life with God at their side. I encouraged them to seek God's forgiveness lifting them up when they fall. I told them life is short and precious to be trapped and bound in the chains of sin and guilt. It is not us who have the power to end our lives but it is God. I encouraged them to embrace God in their daily existence, appreciative that life is beautiful. Rich people will offer millions to anyone who can eradicate death and extend life. I reminded them everything comes from God, belongs to Him and will return to Him. This is the time of giving themselves to Him as love, comfort and life.

Reflection:

There are times in this kind of ministry, you feel bored, sick and less enthusiastic. I'm aware these are distractions from the evil one. This is my prayer, Lord, ablaze me with your fire, keep it burning inside me. Let no one or anything prevent me from serving you. Lord, have mercy on me, a sinner.

There was a woman who was confined due to a vehicular accident. From the looks of it, I could see her battered body and legs. She was in enormous pain, could not move and has to be given pain killers. There was a priest nearby. I asked her if she wants to be anointed with the sacrament of the sick, and she said, yes. I called the priest and she was accorded with the sacrament. When I returned a week later, I found her sitting in a chair, cheerful and could readily move with ease going to the comfort room.[13] She attributed her improvement to a miracle.

There have been people who I have not seen for quite a time. But at some point, I see them confined at Sotto. One was a college batch mate who I haven't seen for close to 40 years who was admitted with an unknown illness. I was attending to other patients when he called my name. He asked me if I recognized him and told him I cannot due to the change in his appearance. He was frail and has matured. I recognized him only when he introduced himself. He told me his health deteriorated when he cut an old tree[14] in their property in Toledo City.[15] He had a hard time eating, sleeping and had been experiencing pain in his body. The doctors could not determine his illness. I encouraged him to undergo confession. I told him his confinement is a time for reflection, how he has been doing in his relationship with God and others.

He admitted there was a time he lost faith in God. He shared his story that some time ago, when he was in the company of soldiers in Mindanao,[16] they were having a drinking spree and they bought

---

[13] A comfort room means a toilet. It is a common word used in the Philippines.

[14] To cut an old tree is one of the more common superstitious beliefs among Filipinos that brings ailment when the cutter has not asked permission from the 'owner' or spirit of the old tree. A ritual has to be done to get permission such as offering blood of a native free range chicken, among others.

[15] Toledo City is a third income class component city in the Province of Cebu, Philippines formerly known as Pueblo Hinulawan. According to the 2015 census, it has a population of 170,335.

[16] Mindanao is another major island in southern Philippines with its largest city, Davao. Mindanao features different tribes and indigenous peoples. It is known for deployment of military personnel because it is the "seat" of conflicts because the island is known to be the "least priority" in government support

a basket of *balut*[17] from a vendor. But they could not eat the eggs as these were rotten and smelly. This angered them and vowed getting even with the vendor. They caught the vendor the next day and shot him several times. He aimed his gun but could not pull the trigger because his conscience dictated it was wrong. This made him realize the existence of God and made him aware that life is sacred. He decided to come back to Cebu, straighten his life until the incident happened in Toledo.

I told him one can change even how sinful he is and there is fulfillment in life walking with God. The sanctifying grace that we receive will change us into true children of God revealing our purpose in life to know, love and serve Him. I told him my walk with God was not easy. The deeper the sins that we commit, the deeper the trials we have. It's either we continue or leave. Many failed to grasp the true meaning of conversion. The purpose of our trials is to strip us of our garbage, impurities and sins and be cleansed with His blood. All the negatives will be converted into positives in the eyes of the Lord. Our hate will be turned to love; lust to purity; weakness to strength; materialism to contentment. I prayed for his conversion and I have not seen him since.

One time, in one of my hospital visits, I saw a former co-employee who I was working with in a furniture export company. He was

---

and services. For more than four decades, Moro groups have been engaged in an insurgency in the island of Mindanao. There have been constant peace talks with the Moro Islamic Liberation Front (MILF), Moro National Liberation Front (MNLF), the Communist Party of the Philippines-New People's Army (CPP-NPA), and the Bangsa Moro Islamic Freedom Fighters (BIFF). Mindanao also is the turf of the terrorist group, Abu Sayyaf, an Islamist militant group based in and around Jolo and Basilan islands in the southwestern part of the Philippines, known for kidnappings-for-ransom cases.

[17] Balut is a boiled egg from a developing bird embryo that is eaten from the shell. It originates in the Philippines and is commonly sold by vendors as street-food. It is common food in Southeast Asia, such as Laos, Cambodia, Thailand and Vietnam.

surprised seeing me in the hospital and inquired who told me of his confinement. I told him, it's God and he laughed aloud. I told him nobody told me of his confinement and told him of my routine on Sundays visiting sick people, talking about God. He was not convinced, aware of my sinful life when I was younger. I opened my bag, showed him rosaries and confessional guides which I later shared with him. I told him I'm so grateful for the opportunity knowing God even as a late comer. I encouraged him to include God in his life. I told him the presence of God in me every day has given me peace of mind and trust in His providence. I explained that being with Him is a prelude of living heaven on earth, where we are destined to be with Him in the next world. His graces are bountiful for those who have given much to Him.

He was my friend, this fireman assigned in the fire department near our place. He married a girl near his workplace and this relationship was not favorably approved by his in-laws. He was noted for his vices and of being a womanizer. He was 30 years old, good looking, muscular as he frequents body building at the gym. I learned he was in and out of the hospital. I had the chance seeing him in the church together with his wife and son. I commented that this was the first time I saw him there and he said he had no choice because he had cancer. He said it started as a small lump on his right leg and became big. He was operated, was biopsied and it was found to be cancerous. He was subjected to chemotherapy and was confined in private hospitals draining the family resources. His in-laws had a change of heart and helped foot the medical bills in the long run.

I was at Sotto when a neighbor told me my friend, the fireman was confined. They didn't have any choice but to admit him in a government hospital due to the expenses. When I saw him, he was pale and very weak. The medication didn't respond to his condition. I told him he needs nourishment, encouraged him to eat more. He replied he lost his appetite and vomits whenever he takes in food. I felt he was nearing death. He told me he had made amends with God aware that he will not last long. I felt pity, and didn't know why I embraced him. I prayed to God for forgiveness and acceptance. A few hours after I left, he died.

Reflection:

I reflected on what happened drawing a conclusion that if everyone will have a balance in life by aligning themselves with God, living and walking with Him up to the end, there will be no fretting out, no fear of death and no trying hard calling for God's help when the candle of existence is soon to extinguish. I believe God will not abandon His people in the hour of death.

I remember the story of my Dad whose friend was a famous physician, successful in his career, owned several landholdings but didn't believe in God. When he was confined in the hospital and nearing death, my father visited him and noticed he was raising his hands up to the air as if calling on a spiritual deity. My Dad inquired, "Why are you calling on some being when in fact you don't believe in God?" His friend answered, he compares his situation to a passenger aboard a sinking ship about to die, and he tries all possible means of survival. Apparently, he didn't survive.

There was a time when no resident priest was available in the hospital. One has to call a priest from a nearby parish tasked of caring to the spiritual needs of patients in providing confession and anointing of the sick. I reminded those who were attending to patients to let them undergo the sacraments considering their patients are in worse condition. I noticed not all patients availed of the sacraments due to lack of priests who are also occupied with other tasks in their respective parishes. But I realized that those who walk with God and are faithful to him who availed of the sacraments before being discharged from the hospital or before they have died. I got this information from the other patients in my next succeeding visits. Indeed, God does not abandon His children in their hour of need and death.

I felt the need of having a resident priest stationed in Sotto administering to the spiritual needs of the patients. I didn't know where to refer this matter. One afternoon after my hospital visit, I decided going to the Archbishop's Palace[18] at D. Jakosalem Street, without any appointment. I had to confer the matter to higher Church authorities. I easily entered the building and knocked on one of the doors of a conference room.

I opened the door and saw people having a meeting and in the center table I recognized Ricardo Cardinal Vidal. Everybody looked at me. I humbly motioned to Cardinal Vidal if I could talk to him. He stood up, went out of the room and conferred with me. I introduced myself and spelled out my concern on the need of having a resident priest assigned at Sotto considering the volume of patients confined there. He told me he will look into the matter. I thanked him and left. A month later, the hospital had a resident priest.

One time, I visited the Gynecological Section at Sotto at a time when this was located at the rightwing fronting the hospital. I administered to a lady from Danao City[19] who was admitted for bleeding. She revealed she was into the illegal gun trade where the guns of different calibers are made in the mountains. I told her this was unlawful in the eyes of God and society. The guns will

---

[18] The Archbishop's Palace is where the Cardinal or the Bishop resides. In Cebu City, this is located at D. Jakosalem Street.

[19] Danao City is a third income class component city in the province of Cebu, Philippines. According to the 2010 census, it has a population of 119,252. It is known for its industry in gun-making.

be used for illegal purposes and instruments in killing. I told her to stop what she was doing. Three months later, I saw her confined again for the same illness. I inquired if she was still into her business, and she replied in the affirmative. I told her God is so patient with us giving us opportunities to mend our ways. I told her chances are, she will always be coming back to the hospital. I told her God will not hesitate ending a life when one is so hard-headed not heeding His call to end sinfulness. I told her time will come when she will be caught by the long arm of the law complicating things like prison and draining of resources. I told her to start a new life with God; let Him direct her life, the purpose and meaning, trust in His providence supplying her daily needs. I never saw her again.

Reflection:

Once you are in this ministry, one must have the gall withstanding all kinds of smell and sight. The time spent at Sotto made me insensitive to different kinds of irritating smell. You get used to seeing broken bodies, detached limbs, fresh wounds and deformities. My regrets are when I see dead bodies wrapped in white blankets destined to the morgue. I grieve when I do not have the opportunity administering to them. I can smell death of those lying unconscious in their beds with apparatus embedded on them. I couldn't talk to them because of their condition. I see them helpless, waiting for the time death will strike them. Several times, I witness family members wail out in outburst, in hysterics when medical personnel fail to revive patients. I seek those who can still hear; who are conscious and maybe nearing death but hopeful in their remaining moments that they can reconcile with God. How I wish God will give me the power to heal; all will witness His glory. They will rise; have a new lease in life when they are reconciled with a loving God. All I can do is utter a prayer, Lord, have mercy on them, let them live.

My contribution is a dot compared to the great works and sacrifices done by known and unknown evangelists, missionaries, and lay people. Mine is only a speck, a tiny fraction. Sometimes, I doubt if this has effect on those I preach. I cannot make a follow-up on them regarding their religious condition. My role is only planting the seed of faith, unaware if this will grow. I trust the Spirit of God will take care of them from the first time I administered, from the present to the future. I pray the seed will be nourished, watered and pruned of unwanted weeds prompting them to grow becoming a big tree, a shade for birds and men. I pray they will walk in righteousness, recipient of God's signs, wonders, miracles and healing.

He was a foreigner of Caucasian descent and was confined due to stab and gunshot wounds but survived. His body was adorned with tattoo and was over 50 years old. His body was heavily bandaged and I noticed that no one was attending to him. I approached him and started a conversation but was immediately turned down because he doesn't want to be bothered and I felt he was suspicious. I continued administering to other patients in the same room. The next week I visited the same ward where he was still confined but didn't approach him. He was observant of what I was doing administering from one patient to the other.

By the third week, I found out that most of the beds were empty and saw him with talking to another patient. They were the ones left. I approached him, smiled and introduced myself again. This time there was a change of heart. He was very attentive and keen on listening while I was talking. I told him he was lucky surviving his ordeal. I told him God loves us. "He allowed you to live because he has unfinished business with you." I told him we cannot be a toughie for the rest of our life dwelling on evil which controls our life. "If you decide continuing what you are doing, you will reap the dire consequences." I told him there is another alternative, the path to goodness. This is possible through the mercy of Jesus Christ who will make the change possible. I told him, "Give your self a chance. Repent your sins; reform your life; shun evil. And I encouraged him to do good things and seek the forgiveness of those he has offended.

I told him life is short and precious; we should not waste it in doing empty things. I told him of the vast opportunities in helping others thereby giving his life a purpose, meaning and lasting peace. I felt he was remorseful as he kept nodding his head.

Reflection:

I find it hard to tell friends about God. I fear they will think of me negatively because most of them are not familiar with my apostolate. There were friends I met but didn't broach the topic about God. I was informed some had died due to sudden illnesses or have succumbed to heart attacks. One worth mentioning was a friend who was a member of the LupongTagapamayapa[20] in our barangay who was more than sixty years old. We shared pancit[21] and bread as snack that evening. I learned he had a heart attack the next morning and was confined at Sotto. I was hopeful I could administer to him revealing Christ into his life. When I visited him

[20] The Lupong Tagapamayapa in the Philippines is the village-based Mediation team who attends to the justice system in the basic local government units, the barangays. Cebu City was once awarded the Best Practice with the village-based mediation with the performance of the barangay-based Lupon Tagapamayapa in 2007. This method of mediation and justice system de-clogs the cases filed in the legal courts. The members of the Lupon Tagapamayapa are volunteers who are trained and given a small stipend. Cases filed with the Lupons are usually settled; otherwise, the parties concerned are free to file cases in the legal courts.

[21] Pancit is food; noodles cooked with sautéed vegetables, spices, meat. It originates from Chinese cuisine.

at the hospital, I was unable to talk to him. He was unconscious and tubes were attached to his mouth and body. Until two weeks' time, he passed away. This has always been the case called as too-late-the-hero. I failed in not sharing him God's love, mercy and forgiveness when there was still time. I resolved from then on to remind friends to have confession, attend Mass regularly, shun sinful life and do good to others.

I invited members of my two prayer communities to become volunteers in the hospital apostolate at Vicente Sotto Memorial Medical Center (VSMMC) in the afternoons of Saturday, Sunday and holidays. I told them we should not be contented in our comfort zones to go to the battle field where the word of God is most needed. I told them the first phase in God's plan is our conversion while the second phase is sharing God's word of salvation to others. This is our call and invited them to join in. There is no pay or honorarium serving Him but it is God who will take care of our needs. I reminded them, the harvest is great; the workers are few and we ask the owner of the harvest to send in more workers. We are the workers he is referring. Unfortunately, no one volunteered. But there are kind- hearted individuals who have supported me in this crusade by contributing rosaries and guides such as Sis. Josie from the University of San Carlos[22] Registrar's Office and Sis. Bebe Ablan of the Alliance of Two Hearts[23].

Lord be gracious to them! I pray for the owner of the harvest sending more workers to the field, reaching out to those who have lost faith, bringing the good news of salvation to their doorstep considering the Church cannot attend to all her sheep. If I'm not

---

[22] The University of San Carlos is a private Catholic university in Cebu City, Philippines administered by the Society of the Divine Word since 1935.

[23] Alliance of Two Hearts is a parish based in Banawa, Cebu City, Philippines.

mistaken, the ratio of one priest is equivalent to thirty thousand parishioners. It's a call for the laity to do its share so members of the flock will not transfer to other religious denominations.

The schedule of my hospital apostolate is done in the afternoons starting at 2 p.m. on Saturdays, Sundays and holidays. I have to skip attending the first Friday vigil at the Alliance of Two Hearts Parish every first week of the month. I miss the vigils where I can give my sharing during my talk on the office assigned to me – the hospital visit apostolate, and listening to those of others. I sleep the whole day on Saturdays after the vigil. I realize those who need the word of Christ are those confined in the hospital and not really the members of my religious community who are always recipient of God's word.

I shared this experience in one of our General Prayer Meetings. And Sis. Alma requested I visit her friend who was confined at Sotto for two weeks due to a serious health problem which I couldn't recall the illness. I learned he was from Mindanao and was employed in one of the biggest department stores in the city. I visited him and found out his condition was worse and expected the worst to come. He had no relatives attending to him but some members of our community took turns in taking care of him. He was so frail and his body was burning with fever and tubes were attached to his body and face. He was expecting me and I prayed over him. I asked God for forgiveness, healing and mercy.

Reflection:

Lord, we offer everything to you. Forgive us of our faults, sins and failures. You are the healer of all healers, doctor of all doctors. You came to this world and healed other sickness. You are the same yesterday, today and tomorrow. Lord, touch his cells, genes, organs, body parts and whole being inside and out. Heal him of his ailment, his physical, mental, spiritual and social faculties. Restore him to his total wellness and being so he will become your servant in the near future. Show mercy to your child and your children who are confined in this hospital.

I bade him goodbye informing him I will attend to the other patients. The next morning, I received a text from Sis. Alma informing me the patient died. I was so devastated, hopeful God in his mercy would make things good. I did ask God, why did you not hear my prayer; admitting my imperfections, at least let him live? Later, upon reflection, I realized, who am I to question God's wisdom? He has reasons why He did not let him live. I asked forgiveness of my poor understanding and outburst.

I administered to a patient of whom the other patient next to him was intensely listening. When I expound on the love of God, the other guy would say, Amen! When I preached the forgiveness of God, he would respond, Amen! This went on until I finished my talk. I went to him and found out he was a Catholic but was converted to Born Again.[24] He was more than 60 years old and resided in the north. I asked him if I could share something to him and not be offended. I told him I knew of somebody older than him who was a Catholic and was converted to another religion. When he sensed his death was near, fear struck him. He called for a priest and had confession. His last instruction to his family in the eventuality of his death is for him to be brought to the Catholic

---

[24] Born Again in the Philippines is a community of Christians whether from Catholic or Protestant denominations who have renewed faith based on the Gospels in the Bible; some of their beliefs also vary in view of the rituals in the celebration of the Holy Mass, the sacraments of the Catholic Church, and their faith intercessions with Mother Mary, the angels and saints.

Church with the Holy Mass accorded with prayers for the departed. I told him to ponder on this.

There was a beautiful woman I visited who was more than thirty years old. She was formerly a Catholic but was converted to another religion when she got married to a pastor. She revealed they had no children prompting her to work in Dubai for quite a time. Accordingly, her past time was spent on drinking, smoking and gambling. There was no spirituality in her but longed for the presence of God. When her yearly physical examination was conducted, she was diagnosed with kidney failure causing the non-renewal of her work contract. While back in Cebu, she was confined in the hospital undergoing kidney dialysis done twice a week.

I inquired if she had misgivings with God. She responded in the affirmative. But later, admitted it was all her fault. She said she has done a lot of sinning and started crying. I reminded her of the love of God; his mercy and forgiveness is available to every repentant sinner. I relayed to her my usual message which she readily accepted. She was amazed why I was there at the right moment when she told her husband five minutes before he left her, the desire of converting back to the Catholic faith. I told her that before I do hospital visit apostolate, I seek God's guidance where He wants me to speak to the patients confined. She was so surprised why I brought up the topic of Mama Mary whom she prayed for the first time in the many years that early morning seeking her intercession. She was thankful of my presence confirming her longings to be closer to God. She resolved to deepen her faith and vowed to preach the good news of salvation to others in her hometown.

I talked with a former neighbor who resettled in Leyte retired from the Philippine National Police (PNP). I encouraged him to repay God for his goodness by serving as a lay minister in his community. This didn't sound a bell to him; he was non-committal but said he will give it a thought. I remembered they had no Christian upbringing in their childhood days and his father was a non-believer. His wife who recently retired as a public school teacher responded positively and offered her services as a catechist serving children during summer.

I administered to a patient who had Stage- 4 throat cancer who was accompanied by his wife. He was operated and advised to undergo chemotherapy. He wrote in a paper with his replies telling me he could not afford the therapy. I learned that he was from Leyte and inquired if he knew my neighbor who was a resident in their place. He said, yes. He knew the retired couple because the husband was his *kumpare* and his drinking partner. He attributed his illness due to booze and smoking. I encourage the couple to offer their lives to God, seeking forgiveness for our sins. I told them God is so gracious giving us time to reconcile with Him. I told them not waste the remaining time we have doing empty things, rather do the works of mercy. The wife revealed she will serve God as a catechist because this was her vocation. I encouraged the husband to do his share by being a prayer warrior. Without his voice, he can pray in behalf of others for their real needs and spiritual conversion. I reminded them we have to recover lost time in our relationship with the Almighty. He wrote my name and promised to convey this message to his *kumpare* that we met and of what I was doing. Perhaps, his *kumpare* will be his first convert.

Reflection:

I met a friend who retired from public service. He told me he is active in his ministry by going to Mindanao where their group is forming chapters for businessmen and professionals. He shared

God has blessed him enormously with needs granted. I said, God be praised! He inquired what I was doing. I told him of the hospital ministry I was serving and he was happy to hear about it because I'm concentrating on the grassroots. But when it came to his graces, I told him it has not rained enormously. I told him of my present financial difficulties borrowing from left to right. I told him the process of survival nowadays is the cycle of borrowing and paying. I told him of the stark reality of having limited paycheck vis-à-vis high prices of commodities and the needs of a growing family. I told him my hair has lessened and by the time my three daughters will go to college, I'll be hairless and bald.

Recently, my wife prepared my recent Sworn Statement of Assets, Liabilities and Networth (SALN) as required of every government employee and she recorded zero in assets, none to personal properties and having liability of loans from the bank. I told him I've been pounding the doors of heaven; until now it has not rained. But I know God is taking care of me and hopeful the day will come God will show mercy allowing a crack on the door where his graces will trickle down giving me relief in breaking the chain of debts which has hounded me ever since. Lord, bless me so I will be a blessing to others.

There was a woman close to 70 years old from the south who was confined. She told me she spent her time in prayer and Bible study early mornings and before going to sleep. What amazed me most was when she started singing in verses. It was soothing, melodious and comforting to hear. I could sense the peace within her and the depth of her faith in God.

Reflection:

When I settled down with my first child, my wife didn't approve I will go to the hospital fearing I will be a carrier of disease which will affect the children. She lamented I should stay in the house during weekends giving quality time to our children. I adhered to what she wanted preventing conflict. I had to take a leave of absence from what I was doing; but inside me, I was uneasy, felt guilty and sad. I had this dilemma for years feeling homesick, nostalgic to serve. My Dad would always inquire if I visited the hospital. I told him not anymore due to my commitment with my family. I had a confession with Fr. Soc of St. Jerome's Learning Center telling him of my problem. He told me I should not feel guilty about it because my apostolate is with my family who needs most of my time and attention. He told me God will have you back anytime. Indeed, God called me back last year when my children could take care of themselves.

One day, I had finished administering to patients at the ground floor of Sotto and was about to leave. I was drawn to the ward on the 2nd floor and was wondering what it will be this time. I went to a lady who was confined; she was around 60 years old. When I asked if I could talk to her, she replied in *Tagalog*.[25] I replied that I'm not well-versed in *Tagalog* and she suggested if we can talk in English. I found out she is from Luzon who migrated to the U.S. and became a citizen. She introduced me to her husband who was half her age. Her business in the U.S. was taking care of the elderly. They were having a holiday in Cebu, having a breakfast of sea food in Mactan, and lunch in Talisay[26] partaking *lechon*. She felt dizzy in the afternoon and the driver of the van brought her to Sotto. She was confined having a mild stroke. I inquired why didn't she transfer to a private hospital and was told that staying

[25] Tagalog is a language; it is the basis of the Filipino, the national language in the Philippines. It is widely spoken in Manila and the Northern parts of the country.
[26] Talisay City is a third income class component city in the province of Cebu, Philippines located in the southern part of the province. It is known for its *lechon* or pigs roasted whole. According to the 2015 census, the city has a population of 227,645.

in a private room is boring. She preferred talking with patients in the ward.

I inquired what were her reflections regarding her confinement. She told me it was great joy helping others. She gave money to the other patients who were in need of medicines, dextrose, food, transportation and other incremental expenses. She revealed she's fortunate having a successful business abroad and vowed sharing her blessings to the less fortunate when she gets back home. She asked her husband to help her in this endeavor, asked him to love her for what she is and not for what she has. She inquired where she can give financial contribution to the hospital. I told her to course this through the hospital chaplain or the administrator. She checked out the next day.

He was from a northern town in the province of Cebu and was admitted due to gunshot wounds in the different parts of his body. From what I gathered, he blacked out while being transported to Sotto and regained consciousness a day later. His occupation was a *traysikad*[27] driver and learned that his own friends were the ones who shot him. I asked him what has he done prompting his friends to kill him. I sensed he was into illegal activities. He was silent and didn't say a word. I told him God has still unfinished business with him and has a purpose why he is still alive. He was sobbing and vowed to do something with his life. He was not married but living with a woman for thirty years. He said he offered marriage but she declined because she belonged to another religion. I told him his relationship is unlawful and at that moment he will have a hard time convincing his live-in partner. I told him she has not been convinced of his sincerity; the way he

---

[27] Traysikads are tricycles assembled in the Philippines; the base is a bicycle designed with a body adding two wheels. Traysikads are driven on foot like bicycles. These are common in side streets and driven on short distances.

has lived his life. He has not shown any change of heart to resolve his own life. If this is possible, then she will have no doubt in her part to say yes to him regarding this matter. I told him the change emanates from him, his behavior, character, outlook in life, commitment to marriage and family. I told him this will be possible if we give our life to Jesus. Nothing is impossible for the greatest sinner to repent, becoming a recipient of a new life Jesus wants us to be. I encouraged him to give his family the change they aspire for, a life of lasting peace and love, marital bliss, aware the father is a changed man. Let them feel that life is not bad. He can do this and the ball is now in his hands.

I saw two personnel from the Bureau of Jail Management and Protection (BJMP) outside the Sotto ward. I knew a prisoner has been confined and sought him for a dialogue. I saw him handcuffed at the side of the bed. I introduced myself; he was very receptive, found out that he was 28 years old and a resident in the city. He was detained due to the drug trade and his case is still in court. He was confined for pneumonia. I asked him if he blames God for his situation; he said, no. He said he is actively a member of a prayer group inside the City Jail and understands that his punishment is his payback time.

At this moment, I shared him my life story.

I told him when I was single, I was into drugs. I was then, one of the managers of a furniture firm in Mandaue[28] and our boss was an American. He calls by phone at 8 a.m., L.A. time which is 12 midnight in our time. He bullshits me on the phone why container vans are not shipped out. I told him you haven't forwarded us

---

[28] Mandaue City is a first income class highly urbanized city in the region of Central Visayas, Philippines. Mandaue City is one of the component cities of Cebu Province located in the central part leading to the north; it is the seat of industries and manufacturing in the Province.

money for the supplies causing the delays in shipment. His calls annoyed me, giving me jitters and I always have a hard time going back to sleep. This led me to skip going home, and spend evenings in night establishments. This indulged me to drink a lot and indulge in substance abuse.

We closed shop when the foreigner deserted us and left us with huge payables. We were sued in court by a lending firm due to bouncing checks. Our lawyer disengaged us when he knew that the foreigner backed out. I learned the imprisonment for bouncing checks is from 6 to 12 months or more depending on the amount involved. This caused me trauma, sleepless nights and the more I indulged on substance abuse. My partner approached his father in-law who was a lawyer seeking assistance on the case. He commented why it took him so long to inform that the incoming verdict is not favorable to us. He said he was confident we could take care of the problem. His father in-law directed him to see the prosecuting lawyer who was incidentally the ninang[29] of his recent marriage. He proceeded to the lawyer's house together with his wife. The lawyer informed them that the judge will render his decision by next week noting our failure in not attending several court hearings. She added the management of the lending firm is bent on putting us behind bars so that their other customers will not be remiss on their payments. She took pity on us aware that we were simply dummies of the company. She cannot afford seeing our future ruined and behind bars at such a young age. The lawyer initiated an amicable settlement with the lending firm for us to turn over things of value to them, settle the case and forego the interest of the loan. A week later, the lending firm filed a notice of desistance in court signifying their intention not to pursue the case. I felt nails were plucked from my body. It was a

---

[29] Ninang means a female wedding sponsor; the male counterpart is a Ninong. In the Philippines, a newly-wed couple can have 25 pairs of wedding sponsors.

temporary relief considering I had no work, no money left and a bleak future. My consumption with drugs increased, and I had the tendency to be suicidal.

I went to a guidance counselor whom I knew during my high school days seeking for help as he was planning to build a rehabilitation center in a southern town. She knew me and I spelled my problems to her. She told me there are three persons whom you meet when transacting with drugs: the seller, buyer and police. She asked me these questions: What if you will be arrested; do you have five thousand pesos to settle your arrest? What if your arrest will be elevated to the fiscal's office; do you have thirty thousand pesos for settlement? What if you will be detained in jail; can you afford to be photographed with your face printed all over the newspapers the next morning? What if you are committed to a rehabilitation center; do you have sixty thousand pesos to complete the six months' session? What if your mental state is altered; are you willing to go to Sotto's mental ward? She told me to go home and think hard on my predicament.

During this time, a kumpare invited me to a seminar in the Life of the Spirit together with my girlfriend who was to be my future wife. At first, I declined, telling him I attended this before. He was so stubborn and I attended the seminar for three days. I learned that my girlfriend kept praying for me, kneeling from the entrance up to the altar of the church imploring God's mercy for my conversion. I became a regular member of the Bato Balani sa Gugma ni Kristo up to the present, a charismatic community at the Cebu Metropolitan Cathedral. I became a member of the Balaang Banay[30] Foundation, a prayer group headed by a priest administering to healing and deliverance. Indeed, he is a God of

---

[30] Balaang Banay is a Cebuano term that literally means Holy Family; it is a foundation that focuses on Christian Lay Ministry.

mercy, through His amazing grace; I was not confined in a rehabilitation center. He stripped me bare from the produce, effect and influence of sin; cleansed me with His blood, released me from the bondage of addiction and the shackles of self-destruction.

I told the prisoner there is still goodness left in us and continue asking God's grace; whatever the outcome of his case, he will walk with the road less traveled. I told him we had the same offense; unfortunately, he was caught.

As for the lady prosecutor, she became the resident Ombudsman of the city and retired. I saw her in one of the supermarkets and wanted to convey my thanks but could not because she was carrying packages accompanied by her daughter. The time came when she was our speaker on the topic, the conduct of ethical standard for public employees given to supervisors. After her talk, I asked permission if I would be given the floor. I related the incident how she helped us and profusely thanked her. I told everyone if not for her I will not be standing in front of the audience. I prayed and asked God to open the floodgates of heaven, shower her with countless blessings and to her family. Everyone stood up and gave her a standing ovation. I saw tears in her eyes, very appreciative somebody remembered her of her good deed.

Reflection:

It hurts when you cannot help because you have no money for those who are in dire need of help.

I went to the male surgical ward and saw the patient wrapped in a white blanket. He was about 40 years old, receptive when I approached him. I saw him wipe his lips with wet cotton. He was not allowed to eat and drink. He bore gunshot wounds in the different parts of his body. He was confined for two days with nobody attending to him. I learned he was a laborer hauling fruits in one of the public markets in the city. I inquired what on earth has he done prompting them to kill him? He remained silent; I inquired if he knew who wanted to kill him. He replied in the affirmative.

I asked him if he can forgive his assailant; he was silent. I told him to forgive and not to retaliate when he is out of the hospital. I told him it's not us who seek vengeance but it's God for he said, vengeance is mine. I was moved to pity of his predicament and inquired if he had relatives who can help him. He said the nurse is still contacting his relatives in the south. I inquired if he knew of my relative who is in the fruit business. He said yes, and told him I will get in touch, see what I can help. I texted my relative if he knew the patient and replied no help is forthcoming. Accordingly, the patient has not forwarded the money from the proceeds of drug sale. His failure prompted the owner of the drugs to liquidate him. It was fortunate, he survived. My relative revealed they don't want to mess up with the person fearing for their own lives and keep mum on the situation. My relative suggested offering prayers so that help will be forthcoming. Whew! I closed my eyes and said, *Lord, have mercy on him. I commend him to you.*

Reflection:

You feel happy when those you administered appreciate what you are doing. From a mere thank you or positive remark that they will aspire to change their life and live a Christian life; it will give you a big boost they understand God's message.

A female patient who was 60 years old sounded happy and said, "Look he is praying for me, asking God I will be cured and will go home right away."

A construction worker commented, "Your message opened my mind that I have to reform my life, give time to my family and lead them to God."

A female patient in handcuffs said, "If I'll be sentenced to prison for shoplifting, I'll seek forgiveness from the owner of the department store."

A female patient commented, "I'm grateful of your coming; now I know I will do my share recovering lost time."

A male patient who was a member of the Youth for Christ commented, "I will do more field work sharing God's message to the youth in our place."
A female visitor who wore a uniform of the 3rd order visiting a patient said, "This should be the kind of work they ought to do."

One female patient said, "I pray the rosary on certain occasions; but now I will pray the rosary daily with my children."

One male patient lamented, "Woe to me not having confession for the past years; now I am in the verge of death. Where can I find a priest to confess?"
A female patient confined who suffered abuse from the cruelty of her husband during the entire life of their marriage prayed for God's mercy that she can forgive her husband who died few years ago.

The list goes on and on.

I know God will not abandon his children. Our union with him is a prelude how to live this world in God's providence, will continue living with him in the next world. I pray there will be a multiplier effect in the work of evangelization.

I met people who survived death in the hands of those who wanted to kill them. A youth from the southern town of Cebu was shot five times in the head during a disco[31] activity but survived. He was fortunate his wounds were not fatal where bullets grazed the sides of his head.

A woman from a northern town was shot in the neck, shoulders, legs and feet. She stumbled down enabling the assailant to back away thinking she was dead. It was fortunate the wounds were not fatal and survived. She knew who attempted to kill her due to a land dispute.

There was a farmer from the north who was hacked with a bolo in the different parts of his body from the man whom he found out was stealing his farm products. His wounds were deep; the most affected was his throat and he could not talk.

It is this kind of people whom you expect not to forgive the persons who did them harm. Their hate and bitterness are evident; thinking to retaliate once they are out of confinement.

---

[31] Disco is a community dance, usually done in rural areas or even in barangays in cities. A disco is usually held during fiesta celebrations, feasts in honor of a patron saint in a parish.

I remember my Dad would skip the surgical section because he had a hard time convincing aggrieved patients to forgive. On my part, when I inquire if they can forgive the person who did this to you, they gnash their teeth and the usual reply is a big NO. I tell them I understand how they feel but it can complicate matters if they take matters in their hands by seeking revenge. I advise them to seek instead the help of the police. In doing so, the burden inside them will be lifted and at the same time, for them to seek God's intercession for forgiveness and comfort. I tell them it's God who will render justice to all who have erred, when he said, vengeance is mine.

At this point, I experience they have calmed down aware of the consequences if they will take the law by themselves. I remind them of God's love, how he suffered and died for us so our sins so will be forgiven. I tell them this love is unconditional, so awesome, reachable and the most potent force on earth where nothing is impossible for great offenders to be given new lease in lives. I urge them to forgive so that they will be forgiven. I urge them to forgive so that all ill feelings they harbor will be gone. I urge them to forgive so they can savor God's healing, goodness and continue with our lives. I urge them to forgive so they can love the unlovable. As I leave, I see the peace in their faces and I pray to God to transform them into what He wants them to be.

I feel inspired administering to the youth who are confined; I shared this during one of the meetings at the Alliance of Two Hearts. I find this sector naïve, raring to go, daring to experiment on new ideas and activities; and can easily be exploited. I told them of my biggest blunder in life of not knowing Jesus early. I experienced lost time and opportunities due to bad company, vices and indulging in a risky lifestyle. I tell them they should walk the right path to fulfill their dreams and aspiration. It's good if their foundation is paved with discipline. Hard work and love of

God should be instituted by their parents. They can say no to the bad things offered to them. My concern is those who lack parental guidance, weak in character, having low esteem, experiencing vices early, and being happy go lucky. I tell them not to be drawn into what others are doing indulging in booze, drugs and having loose relationships. I tell them not to glamorize these activities because it's not worth being led to self-destruction such as teenage pregnancy, HIV, sexually transmitted infections, crime offending, jail sentence, being a school dropout. I tell them to associate with godly friends and groups who appreciate life, good morals with an advocacy of helping others. I tell them to let God be part of their daily lives for it is He who will direct their studies, careers, relationships, and the future; and no one will go astray. He will send people and opportunities without their knowing for their betterment. Life in Christ is wonderful, full of purpose and meaning, blessings and benefits. I know this because I am a recipient of his generosity even as a late comer.

I went to the non- communicable ward at Sotto. I visited a woman confined in bed whose right foot was heavily bandaged. It was evident her foot was damaged by diabetes. When I talked to her, I noticed her face seems familiar. I remembered she was the owner and cook of the eatery near the furniture export factory I was connected with in Mandaue City during the 90's. She was proficient in her business, cooked delicious meals. When I told her my name, she immediately recognized me. She was surprised seeing me and couldn't believe in what I was doing. She was scheduled for operation anytime of the week and her infected foot will be amputated. I asked her if she ever blamed God for her condition which she replied in the negative. I said we should not blame Him because it's not His doing why we have become diabetic but due to our lifestyle. I told her the loss of her foot is not the end of the world and this is the time for embracing God in a deeper way, understanding His will in our life. I said whatever we lack in the Lord, we add.

I shared to her what I had done after I left the furniture factory. I told her of my conversion, my walk with God, my work, my family and my mission and that we must do our share in telling others the love of God whatever condition we are in. I gave her a copy of the confessional guide, requested from her the daily recitation of the holy rosary, and requested the resident priest that she undergoes the sacraments before her scheduled operation. I left her cheerful not fearful of the future with one left foot left.

He was about 30 years old, single and confined due to gunshot wounds. He was a security guard, was shot while manning his post one early morning. He didn't know why he was shot recalling he had no altercation with anybody. He told me his wounds were damaging his spinal column causing him not to walk anymore. I find it hard consoling him not knowing if my message would have an effect on his grave condition. I had doubts letting him understand God's message. I prayed to God for the right words to come out of my mouth so he can comprehend. I slowly told him of a forgiving God who forgives us and not remembering our sins. I told him of a compassionate God who understands our needs and sufferings. I told him of a loving God who loves us so much that he will not abandon and forsake us. I told him of a merciful, healing God; when man cannot do the impossible, He can make it possible. I told him whatever the outcome of our condition, answered prayer or not, to ask God to make us a good person. I left him unsure of what his future will be but I trust an all forgiving, compassionate, loving, merciful and healing God will take care of him.

When I finished administering to a patient at Ward 9, a guy tapped me at the back requesting that I give confession to his ailing mother. As I approached the bed, I noticed the mother was more than 70 years old. The husband beside her was of the same age and they were surrounded by their sons and daughters. I learned that they are from the north of Cebu. I informed them that I was not a priest and that a resident priest is available upon request who gives confession, as well as the anointing of the sick and that his office is located in the second floor. I told them that it's not only their mother who needs this sacrament but all of them because they are one family and part of her healing.

With this opening statement, I proceeded with my usual conversation. I expounded the need for us to change, integrate God into our daily life and faithfully walk with Him until the end. I told them the importance of the sacrament of reconciliation because God's grace is open to every repentant sinner.

I experienced a similar case before where an acquaintance whose father was confined at the Intensive Care Unit (ICU) in a private hospital. His father lay unconscious for a week and fearful that he will not make it. They required a priest for the anointing of the sick but the priest instead asked the members of the family to undergo confession. My friend revealed he was elated of the priest's request aware that some members of his family were remiss in their faith. Accordingly, the confession took more than an hour and finally the priest administered the sacrament of extreme unction. An hour after the priest left, they noticed movement in the patient's hands. After three days, the father checked out from the hospital. The incident encouraged family members to renew their faith in God and their relationship with one another.

I did not know the result of the outcome of the mother of the family I administered but was hopeful with God's grace, things would turn out right.

Those serving God should practice what they preach. This is a reminder for those serving 'hands on' with God.

He was more than 50 years old from Bohol[32] province and was confined due to abdominal pain. He told me this was the first time he was confined in a hospital. He revealed he was an active lay minister in his place and instrumental in the formation of the different charismatic groups in his locality. I told him his stay there is a break from his busy schedule. I told him it is an opportunity reflecting how far we have gone in our service, what is lacking, what has to be added and a self-reflection of our life. He admitted he was active in his ministry but enjoyed past time. He was with constant drinking spree with friends and could not say no to them. He tried to stop his vice but failed and has always been visible in public, so drunk. He realized he was a bad example in the community as a servant of God noting that the prayer groups he set up died a natural death. He realized his actions were detrimental to those who want to renew their faith in God. He was thankful realizing his failure and vowed becoming a changed person God wants him to be.

He was confined due to gunshot wounds and was fighting for his life but survived. He was over 30 years old, a resident of the city and was hit by gunfire while staring at a guy past midnight after work. When I talked to him about God's mercy, he laughed at me and asked, "Is it not awkward asking God's help when most of my life I did not believe Him? What can I expect from Him when I do not know Him?" I told him God's mercy is open to all, especially to a repentant sinner. I told him this is the time to open his heart and accept Him as Lord and Savior. I told him to be humble, to cast all his doubts and ask God to strengthen his faith because in this kind of situation, we all need Divine Providence. I noted that

---

[32] Bohol is another province located in Central Visayas Philippines.

nobody was attending to him.[33] He revealed he has an aunt in a convent and I told him I will relay the message of his confinement. The next day, I left a message for the nun in this convent he specified hoping that she could drop by and inspire him to know and trust his life to a loving God.

One time I said, Lord I have covered much and I have to leave because I have to attend Mass at 5:30 p.m. But when I was about to exit from Ward 9, I was drawn to a guy who was confined; he was sitting on his bed conversing with her teenage daughter and a woman was sleeping in his bed beside him. I made my talk and he was listening intently. He was more than 50 years old and was from northern Cebu. He told me he was separated from his wife and the woman sleeping beside him is his common-law-wife. I told him I had been to his place in the past when I was a teenager and he confirmed the names of my friends and told me that they are still there. I told him I was staying in the house of my uncle during vacation and at this moment, his common-law-wife woke up and said that she heard some of our conversation. She said my uncle was her father-in-law whose eldest son, my cousin became her legal husband. They had a5 children but unfortunately parted ways because her husband had other families. She said that her husband's health condition is deteriorating due to excessive drinking and is living in with a younger woman.

I told them this was possible because her husband had plenty of money as he worked abroad as a seaman.[34] Similarly, their own

---

[33] It is very common in the hospitals in the Philippines that patients have people who attend to them other than the medical personnel. Attending means to keep them company and they may be family members, relatives, friends or neighbors.

34 It is common knowledge in the Philippines that usually seamen employed abroad are offered hefty salaries in dollars or other currencies. It is also a usual pattern for seamen to have more families other than their legal spouses.

children who got married also suffered the same fate of separation from their spouses. I told them my uncle, who also worked as a seaman also had other children from other women. Even before he died, there was such disarray among siblings and children who have separated from their spouses or partners. I told them relationships become dysfunctional due to parental neglect and I was not surprised that the same thing happened to her and the husband who was my cousin. I find it hard for them to be together in holy matrimony considering the complication of their past marriages which entails high cost in litigation for annulment. But I encouraged them to do good always in spite of their condition and to follow God to the end.

Reflection:

There are things I have done but did not know what the consequences of my actions have been. It would have been better Lord, if you cautioned me from my comments so as not to complicate things. But there have been times when I believe that I am right; I express my sentiments and air my grievances when truth is trampled upon.

You know the doings of men, good or bad. Nothing is hidden from You and You will strengthen what has been unjustly done. I offer my life into your hands, trustful in you Lord that you will not abandon me. You will protect me from evil, danger and injustice all the days of my life. You will chart my future, guide me in my work; give me strength in this apostolate with you, with others and with my family. You will be gracious in my need; comfort me in my worries and console me from my uncertainties for You are in control of everything. I am dependent in Your Spirit who will teach me how to pray, who knows the will of God in my life, who helps me carry my cross daily and I may live a Christian life. Your Spirit will be my comfort, my friend, my helper, my teacher, my counselor and giver of generous gifts. In my nothingness, I give my life to you entirely and completely.

Jesus, show me Your mercy and compassion and let me be humble always; not boastful, bragging, feeling more spiritually better than others. Help me not to judge others in their inadequacy of faith. Let my work inspire others to do the same bringing them to You. Let me shun temptation, evil and lures of the world which will separate me from You. Let me be meek in my ways, soft in words and dutiful in work and family. Let the fire keep burning through Your Spirit doing what is good and just. Embrace me with your loving arms against adversities and temptations that come my way.

Give us opportunities of helping others. Instill Your Holy Presence in our walk with You mindful of your peace, love and grace. There is one thing that I fear most; don't leave me Lord. I need you in my life. I don't know what the future will bring. In you my Lord, we will be fully alive, perfectly healthy, overflowing with peace, overflowing with joy, radiating in power, radiating in holiness, enjoying super abundant blessings and serving you joyfully.

Most of the time we do everything by ourselves; so trustful that we don't need God in our life. We remember Him on occasions on Sundays, celebrations of the church and days of obligation. Once fulfilled, we do things on our own even those that are not right. We think God as a mere symbol, an obligation and relic. We call upon Him when we are in trouble. We are not aware He wants to be a part of our life, to walk with Him every day, do and follow His will and share in the work of evangelization so others may know Him. We only come to our senses when things are not favorable on our side, when we cannot do anything, and worse, we suffer. He allows trials to happen prompting us to call on Him, seek forgiveness and healing. Why do we suffer? Jesus was not spared from suffering but conquered it including death. We are all imperfect. There is so much imperfection of this world where we live in. Perfection will be realized once we are with Him in the next world. The adversities He allows will give us an insight that He is in control of everything. We need Him most when we are down and out. The sufferings offered to Him by His mercy will turn to gems, transforming to greater gifts.

A friend sent this text message in my mobile phone: It's our daily battles offered to Him that will make us winners; the fights and struggles we undertake with His help will steer us to victory. Our problems offered to Him will reveal His greatness. The brokenness we suffered offered to Him will make us whole. The avenue of His miracles and blessings will be realized if we can sustain the hardest and most painful things through His grace.

My walk at Sotto has made me appreciate life, realizing its meaning and purpose; the realization of giving my utmost for others. I'm thankful how blessed I am even in my inadequacies. There are times I doubt His generosity, why some have more than everything they need. My walk at Sotto revealed I'm blessed, thankful I'm walking while those I administer are lying down, frightful of their condition while most are in pain. I was not mistaken in my decision offering my life to a loving God. This was the turning point in my life. His total love changed me, loosened me up, healed me and empowered me to serve. I learned contentment in my limitations and grateful of His daily supplications. I am happy of my wellbeing in spite of having controllable illnesses. His grace has been sufficient lifting me when I fall. My walk with Him led me to a deeper faith, gave me a tongue that speaks about healing and life. I thank you, Father, for giving me the greatest gift of all, your son, Jesus Christ.

I never knew You before but had only a glimpse of Your life. I was distant, away from you and sinned a lot. You had to admonish me of my sinfulness. You stripped me of everything not knowing where to go. I had to seek You asking help hoping that what I lost will be restored. Your ways are different from what I expected. You allowed trials to consume me if I remain or leave. It was hard to understand why one has to undergo continuous suffering. But Your grace made me sustain my faith. The cleansing process took long and hard. There were times when I cried out when it will end. I survived the ordeal sanitizing my garbage, filth and junk of the long years accumulated. If not for your mercy I could not survive, and continue my walk with you in these trying times.

Lord, thank you for the gift of life. Thank you for faith, prayer, forgiveness, the Church and sacraments, this work, creation and my family.

Lord, thank you for giving me the opportunity of knowing, loving and serving You. Thank you for embracing, guiding and caring for me against the ills of the world. In my emptiness, I kneel down in your feet for mercy.

I am asking God to make it possible that this witnessing and walk at Sotto with this apostolate will see print. I am assisted by an amiable colleague, Malou Alorro who works at the Cebu City Sangguniang Panlungsod[35] Secretariat Office to endorse for publishing. My intention is He will be known, not me, considering that this ministry needs workers who cater to those who need conversion and spiritual healing. I consider it urgent for those who have limited time so that they are accorded with the benefit

---

[35] The Sangguniang Panlungsod literally means City Council of the Legislative Department of a local government unit (LGU).

of reconciliation with a loving God before one's door is completely shut.

Somebody asked me how will I want to be remembered?

I told him, a simple guy who said yes to Jesus; did what he was told and will continue doing more.

Hospital del Sur constructed in 1911 during the American Occupation in Cebu, Philippines.

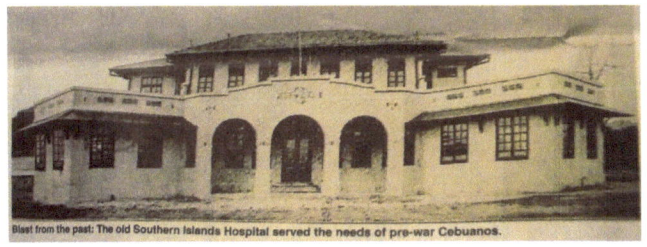

Renamed as Southern Islands Hospital in 1913.